PAST & PRESENT

CARMEL-BY-THE-SEA

Opposite: The Pine Inn hotel stands alone on the north side of Ocean Avenue between Monte Verde and Lincoln Streets around 1908. The view, looking west toward Carmel Bay, shows numerous newly planted pine trees along Ocean Avenue. Carmel-by-the-Sea has often been described as a village in the forest by the sea. (Courtesy of Henry Meade Williams Local History Room, Harrison Memorial Library, Carmel, California.)

PAST & PRESENT

CARMEL-BY-THE-SEA

Alissandra Dramov

"We shape our buildings, and afterwards our buildings shape us."

—Winston Churchill,
House of Commons speech, October 28, 1943

ON THE FRONT COVER: The majestic Cypress Inn began as Hotel La Ribera in 1929. Located at the northeast corner of Lincoln Street and Seventh Avenue, the historic hotel was co-owned by legendary Hollywood entertainer and Carmel resident Doris Day for over three decades. (Past image, courtesy of Henry Meade Williams Local History Room, Harrison Memorial Library, Carmel, California; present image, author's collection.)

ON THE BACK COVER: This historic view of the intersection of Dolores Street and Seventh Avenue looking north toward Ocean Avenue in the 1930s shows what was the heart of downtown Carmel-by-the-Sea for more than a generation, from the 1920s through the 1950s. (Courtesy of Henry Meade Williams Local History Room, Harrison Memorial Library, Carmel, California.)

CONTENTS

ACKNOWLEDGMENTS

First, I would like to thank Carmel-by-the-Sea's Harrison Memorial Library local history librarian Katie O'Connell for all her assistance in locating the majority of the historic photographs used in this book. Unless otherwise noted, all historic photographs are courtesy of the Henry Meade Williams Local History Room, Harrison Memorial Library, Carmel, California. Thank you also to James Perry, executive director of the Monterey County Historical Society, and Jennifer Smith, local history and special projects librarian of the Monterey County Free Libraries, for their assistance. All modern-day photographs are by the author.

Additionally, I would like to express my appreciation and admiration of the numerous volunteers in the community who serve our village in so many tangible ways. They take the initiative in maintaining Carmel's character, keeping the village true to its founders' roots and protecting the town's beauty and aesthetics, led by members of Carmel Cares, Carmel Residents Association, and Carmel Preservation Association.

Last, an explanation of Carmel's unusual way of designating locations. There are no street numbers in Carmel-by-the-Sea, so addresses are given geographically based on the four cardinal points—north, east, south, and west—of the intersection of two streets.

INTRODUCTION

Carmel-by-the-Sea has been described as a village in the forest by the sea, noted for its many pine and cypress trees, its beautiful white sandy beach, and its comfortable, year-round Mediterranean climate. *Architectural Digest* called it the prettiest town in California. The small coastal community covers one square mile along the Pacific, 120 miles south of San Francisco. Carmel-by-the-Sea's origins go back to the establishment of the Carmel Mission in 1771. The first short-lived real estate development was Carmel City, a Catholic summer resort in the late 1880s set up by Monterey real estate developer S.J. Duckworth, which failed in the economic downturn of the 1890s.

At the start of the 1900s, the next real estate development would be successful. Carmel-by-the-Sea began with the establishment of the Carmel Development Company in 1902 by San Francisco lawyer Frank Powers and Santa Clara Valley real estate developer Frank Devendorf. The new community was ingeniously marketed as a Bohemian artists' and writers' colony and has maintained its cultural emphasis on art, writing, and performing arts since its earliest days. Devendorf and Powers boasted that prominent intellectuals, professors, writers, artists, and poets were drawn to Carmel-by-the-Sea as a place where they could afford a small lot for a simple redwood bungalow and focus on creative pursuits through the inspiration of the surrounding Arcadian paradise with its mild temperatures and beautiful natural surroundings.

Early on, Frank Devendorf gave away and planted thousands of pine trees across the town. His legacy initiated Carmel's love and protection of trees in its urban forest that thrives to this day. In the founding years, the town consisted mostly of residential cottages built with natural materials such as wood and stone, made to fit into the site and blend into the landscape. The few stores along the main street, Ocean Avenue, sprang up to provide the basics. Carmel-by-the-Sea had dusty dirt roads until the 1920s and no electricity until the 1910s. The city was incorporated in 1916.

The first period of growth began in the 1920s through the 1930s, when affluent new residents arrived and built vacation homes, where they spent part of the year. More retail stores were established downtown, with businesses that provided services for residents. A sizable number of these historic buildings survive and are the core of Carmel-by-the-Sea's downtown. Most of the early Western false front and some of the Craftsman styles were replaced by European Revival styles that defined the look of the downtown and gave it a quaint European charm.

The 1920s were a pivotal time when the town defined itself and its approach to growth with the establishment of a planning commission (1922) and zoning laws. Key battles over development emerged that demarcated two opposing sides: art versus business; i.e., the Bohemians versus the businessmen. The soul of Carmel was solidified by Ordinance No. 96 in 1929, which stated the town is primarily a residential community, with business and commerce forever subordinate in the past, present, and future. This statement of Carmel-by-the-Sea's foremost residential character is still so vital to defining the town that it is framed on the wall at city hall's council chambers. Carmel's champion at the time was journalist Perry Newberry, who was mayor in 1922. He adamantly fought to preserve Carmel's beauty, artistic character, and community against forces of growth, commercialism, and "progress." He was a leader in the Don't Pave Main Street movement of 1922 and in preventing commercial development along Carmel's scenic coastline and beach.

The second period of growth and influx of domestic tourism was post–World War II in the 1950s with an increase in automobile travel due to the newly constructed interstate highway system and postwar economic boom. Downtown businesses shifted focus to tourists, with an emphasis on commercialism, the hospitality industry, more art galleries, and retail shops that sold souvenirs over the everyday needs of residents. Resistance to modern architecture and massive development plans, such as large hotels and the town's first shopping mall, the outdoor Carmel Plaza (1960), defined the battles of the time, as these projects were seen as out of scale and out of character with Carmel-by-the-Sea.

The third period of growth and wave of international tourism was in the 1980s largely due to the national and global publicity from the election of Hollywood actor and resident Clint Eastwood as mayor in 1986. This brought in large numbers of visitors who came with the hopes of catching a glimpse of the star at city hall or his downtown restaurant, Hog's Breath Inn. Increased growth and development created a backlash that led to a burst of preservationist activity to save homes and buildings from being torn down, combined with efforts to document Carmel's historic structures, spearheaded by activist Enid Sales. By the late 1990s, the city compiled an inventory of 300 historic houses and buildings, which are protected by state and local laws.

Present-day controversy is centered around concern over real estate developers who purchase entire city blocks or multiple adjacent lots to tear down existing structures and plan for new mega-scale projects, which some residents say do not fit into the town. Resistance also continues to modern architecture, as opponents say the size and style of these structures appear out of place with Carmel and its architectural traditions.

Carmel-by-the-Sea is a small community of just over 3,200. Its quaint and quirky charm is celebrated and preserved, such as the lack of street numbers, no home mail delivery, no streetlights downtown nor in the residential neighborhoods, no residential sidewalks, no fast food, no chain stores or chain hotels, no parking meters, no electric traffic signals, no neon signs, no billboards, no industry or manufacturing, and no commercial development along the scenic coast.

The key to understanding the town and its history is to comprehend the persistence of a strong current of resistance to change, growth, development, and commercialism that has existed since its beginning days. Carmel's residents are passionate and outspoken. The city prides itself on being different and staying true to its founders' ideals. Residents through the years have consistently fought to keep it unique, special, and one of a kind and to defend it against forces that seek to undo these qualities. Every generation has had its heroes who stood up for preserving the town and keeping its integrity as its founders had envisioned.

Locals, along with regional, national, and international visitors, love Carmel-by-the-Sea for its distinctive, unparalleled qualities. The scenic, picturesque, charming town reminds people of a European village with its delightful cottages, distinguishing architecture, stone-and-brick-lined passageways and courtyards, many trees, and sandy beach. The town's layout and landscape encourage exploration and walking. Its dog friendliness is renowned and unsurpassed. These factors all contribute to its unrivaled sense of place. *Travel + Leisure* magazine readers in 2020 voted Carmel in the top 15 US cities; it was the only city from California and from the entire West Coast on the list. People live in and visit the town as it provides an escape from the everyday, mundane, outside, high-tech, Anytown USA, cookie-cutter world. Carmel's resistance to change has preserved its unique, incomparable qualities and is what most attracts people to it—what its residents have fought for and vigilantly maintained through the years.

CHAPTER 1

OUTDOORS

Monterey real estate developer Santiago J. Duckworth established the short-lived Carmel City in the 1880s as a Catholic summer resort. He is shown in this c. 1890 photograph seated in a horse cart in the northeast part of town on the Lower Trail overlooking Carpenter Street. Looking to the southwest, Carmel Bay and Point Lobos are in the distance.

Built in 1889 on the beach at the foot of Ocean Avenue, Carmel's bathhouse was one of the earliest buildings constructed in Carmel City. The wood structure with a ribbon of glass windows facing Carmel Bay, shown in 1922, was a social gathering place for years—where club meetings, parties, and dances were held and one could buy a snack, rent a swimsuit, or gather to watch the stormy waves. After falling into disrepair in the 1920s, the bathhouse was torn down in 1929.

Carmel's Forest Theater was the third open-air theater in the West when it was constructed in 1910; the others were Northern California's Bohemian Grove and the University of California Berkeley's Greek Theater. The historic photograph is from 1912. Bohemian thespian—later businessman and mayor—Herbert Heron (1883–1968) founded it on a city block provided by the Carmel Development Company on the northeast corner of Santa Rita Street and Mountain View Avenue. From the early years, productions fostered community spirit and further promoted Carmel-by-the-Sea as an artistic and cultural town.

In 1922, the City of Carmel-by-the-Sea held its first bond issue. It passed, and the city bought the sand dunes from the Carmel Development Company to prevent commercial development along the beach. As part of the deal, the cofounder of the Carmel Development Company, Frank Devendorf (1856–1934), included for free Block 69, an entire city block at the entrance to town between Junipero and Mission Streets and Ocean and Sixth Avenues. This view shows what became the park entrance at Ocean Avenue, looking north.

Two civic-minded women, Mattie Hopper, wife of writer Jimmy Hopper, and Clara Kellogg, a progressive activist and council member, led the block's beautification efforts starting in 1928. The land became a city park in 1930. After landscaping with grass, shrubs, and trees and constructing a fishpond and low flagstone border wall, it was named Devendorf Park in Frank Devendorf's honor in 1932. It is seen here shortly after it opened. The view is looking west. Through the years, several commemorative memorial markers were added.

The c. 1908 photograph shows horseback riders gathered at the old horse watering trough in the busy center of town at the intersection of Ocean Avenue and San Carlos Street. The World War I Memorial Arch was built at this location; ground breaking occurred on November 11, 1921. The flagstone, Spanish Mission Revival–style memorial at the center median divider was designed in 1919 by prominent Southern California architect Charles Sumner Greene (1868–1957), by then a Carmel resident. The arch was restored in 1977 and 2019.

CHAPTER 2

CHURCHES

In 1917, Carmel's builder, Michael J. (M.J.) Murphy Jr. (1885–1959), constructed the Craftsman-style Christian Science church on Monte Verde Street and Fifth Avenue, seen here in 1918. It was later taken apart and moved to Santa Rita Street and Fifth Avenue to spare it from demolition, and it became a residence. A new church built in 1950 on Monte Verde Street near Sixth Avenue now too faces the threat of demolition.

The unique Tudor Revival, Storybook-substyle one-story building with a turret and steeply pitched side gable roof was constructed on the south side of Ocean Avenue east of Monte Verde Street in 1923 as part of the Golden Bough complex. It was designed for Herbert Heron by Edward G. Kuster (1878–1961), who established the Court of the Golden Bough, and was constructed by M.J. Murphy. In the 1930s, the building was the Christian Science reading room. Since then, it has been a retail shop.

All Saints' Episcopal Church was constructed in 1913 on the east side of Monte Verde Street between Ocean and Seventh Avenues. San Francisco architect Albert Cauldwell's original wood-shingled, Craftsman-style design with a steep-pitched gable roof is seen in the 1915 photograph. M.J. Murphy was the builder. The City of Carmel-by-the-Sea bought the building in 1946 and repurposed it as the new city hall. Design changes included the flat-roofed classical portico entry addition to the council chambers in 1953.

The Carmel Mission on Rio Road celebrated its 250th anniversary in 2021. Headquarters for the California missions, it was founded by Franciscan missionary Fr. (now Saint) Junipero Serra (1713–1784), who died and is buried at the mission. The stone church built in 1797 fell into disrepair in the 1850s, and the roof collapsed. In 1884, a steep, high-pitched roof (an incorrect style) was put in, seen in the 1928 photograph. Harry Downie's 1930s renovation brought an arched ceiling and proper low-pitched, handmade tile roof replacement. (Past image, courtesy of Library of Congress.)

The back of the Carmel Mission on Lausen Drive is shown in this undated historic photograph; additional buildings now surround it. Mission San Carlos Borromeo del Río Carmelo was originally established in 1770 in Monterey but was moved in 1771 to be closer to fertile land and a water source, the Carmel River, hence the name. The mission was surrounded by orchards, dairy, and ranch land. The mission property is now a state and national historic landmark and is listed in the National Register of Historic Places. (Past image, courtesy of Library of Congress.)

Carmel's first Protestant church was the Methodist church on the west side of Lincoln Street north of Seventh Avenue. The c. 1905 Spanish Mission Revival–style building is shown shortly after it was constructed. A new church designed by architect Robert Stanton (1900–1983) replaced the original one at the same location, constructed in 1940 and renamed Church of the Wayfarer. The church, which has a Shoenstein organ, custom-made stained-glass windows, and a biblical garden, is a popular wedding location.

CHAPTER 3

HOTELS AND RESTAURANTS

OCEAN AVENUE, CARMEL BY THE SEA, CALIF.

The north side of Ocean Avenue at San Carlos Street looking west toward Carmel Bay is shown in this postcard around 1909. The large, two-story, wood-shingled Hotel Carmel with its sunporch is on the right. It was Carmel City's second oldest hotel, built in 1898. It burned down in 1931 and was replaced by the Spanish Colonial Revival–style Goold Building.

The two-story, Craftsman-style Hotel Carmelo, built in 1889, the first hotel constructed in Carmel City, is seen in 1903 at its original location on the northeast corner of Ocean Avenue and Junipero Street near the entrance to downtown, before it was moved west five city blocks and became the Pine Inn. The old location became a livery stable, then the Village Inn, a historic hotel built in 1954 by architect James Pruitt (1912–1986) of Comstock Associates, now renamed The Getaway.

HOTELS AND RESTAURANTS

When the Hotel Carmelo was moved using horses and log rollers several city blocks to the north side of Ocean Avenue at Monte Verde Street in 1903, it was enlarged with the addition of an entrance, sunroom, dining room, and stable, and renamed the Pine Inn. A tent ground was set up around the hotel to house excess guests, as seen in this early view from 1904, which also shows the new annex in the foreground. The Pine Inn is Carmel-by-the-Sea's oldest hotel.

Pine Inn
Carmel by the Sea, Calif.

The Pine Inn underwent significant remodels and expansions in the 1920s and 1940s, eventually spanning the entire city block between Ocean and Sixth Avenues and Monte Verde and Lincoln Streets. The late 1920s view shows the hotel after a major architectural remodel by Oakland architects Blaine and Olson into a Spanish Revival style with white stucco exterior, abandoning the previous Craftsman style. Noted designer Jon Konigshofer's (1906–1990) early 1940s remodel saw the addition of a rooftop garden outdoor dining area, 12 retail shops, brick walkways, and a pub.

Across the street to the west, Lobos Lodge was established in the 1920s to accommodate extra guests from the Pine Inn. The cabins on the northwest corner of Ocean Avenue and Monte Verde Street offered weekly and summer rentals. Lobos Lodge was advertised as "Carmel's famous cottage hotel." The original cottages seen in the early view were torn down in the 1970s and completely new and modern units were built, designed by architect Will Shaw (1924–1997). A courtyard, shops, and parking spaces were also constructed.

Lobos Lodge
Carmel-by-the-Sea, Calif.

Zan 510

The Holiday Inn (not part of the hotel chain) began in 1924 as Holiday Inn at the Beach at 2408 Bayview Avenue and Martin Way in Carmel Point, just outside of Carmel-by-the-Sea's southwestern city limits. One famous guest, architect Frank Lloyd Wright (1867–1959), regularly stayed there in the early 1950s while working on Della Walker's now landmark Scenic Road house one block away. Della was the wife of Clinton Walker. The Prairie-style hotel became the Sandpiper Inn in 1970, now undergoing renovation ahead of its centennial anniversary.

Carmel-by-the-Sea's European-inspired architecture is defined by the iconic Tuck Box restaurant, designed in 1926 by Hugh Comstock (1893–1950) in his beloved signature fairy tale Storybook style, reserved for his houses. Built on the east side of Dolores Street north of Seventh Avenue, it began as Sally's restaurant, seen here around 1928, before construction of the Garden Shop and Addition, built respectively in 1929 and 1931. In 1941, it became the Tuck Box, an English tearoom, which celebrated 80 years in business in 2021 and still serves afternoon tea and scones.

Proprietor Agnes Signor leased and then bought artist Chris Jorgensen's stone mansion on Camino Real and Eighth Avenue and turned it into a boardinghouse known as the Strand in 1915. The early Camino Real view was taken in 1921, a year before Signor added 20 guest rooms and made it a full-service hotel called La Playa, Carmel-by-the-Sea's second-oldest hotel. Signor ran it with her nephews Harrison and Frederick Godwin, who eventually became owners. In the 1940s, Harrison owned the Pine Inn, and Fred became mayor.

The 1921 postcard shows the back view of the Strand facing Carmelo Street the year before it became the La Playa hotel. Known fondly as the "Grand Dame of Carmel," the hotel celebrated its centennial in 2005. It is renowned and beloved for its award-winning gardens, swimming pool, and location for weddings, with sweeping views of Carmel Bay from Cypress Point in Pebble Beach to the northwest and Point Lobos to the southwest. It was renamed La Playa Carmel in 2012 under new ownership.

After a Christmas 1924 fire, the hotel was rebuilt and enlarged by M.J. Murphy and reopened in mid-1925. The new hotel entrance is shown. The Craftsman wood-shingled style was replaced with a stucco exterior. La Playa expanded again in the 1940s to the south in a Spanish Revival style. It had 80 rooms along with the southwestern addition of the terrace dining room overlooking Carmel Bay by designer Jon Konigshofer. It now has 75 rooms after a remodel and sale of the presidential suite in 2012, which became a private residence.

La Playa Hotel
Carmel by the Sea, Calif

LA PLAYA HOTEL

A cocktail lounge adjacent to the dining room, designed by Jon Konigshofer, was added to the hotel in the early 1950s. During the 1960s under owner Bud Allen, the "Dime Time" tradition began, a 10-minute happy hour at the full-service bar with drinks for 10¢, which remains to the present day. La Playa continues to be cherished by visitors and locals; it has won the Golden Pine Cone award for Best Hotel by *Carmel Pine Cone* readers multiple times.

Hotel La Ribera was built in 1929 on the northeast corner of Lincoln Street and Seventh Avenue. Print advertisements in the 1930s called it "The Home of Hospitality" and highlighted "steam heated, fireproof, radio connection in all rooms." There were special winter rates, weekly and monthly rates from $50, and a "European plan $2.00 to $8.00 per day." A dining room opened in 1930. The large, elegant Spanish Eclectic–style hotel became the Cypress Inn in the mid-1980s under co-owner Doris Day, who remained as such until her death in 2019.

Cypress Inn has been awarded the Golden Pine Cone as the Most Dog-Friendly Hotel, and Terry's Restaurant & Lounge (named for Doris Day's son) was voted the Most Dog-Friendly Restaurant. The building was designed by Oakland architects Blaine and Olson, who spent two years in Spain studying Spanish architecture. The hotel's central Moorish tower is a defining feature. The original wooden gates to the garden courtyard, now the outdoor dining patio, are seen in the early view, later replaced with wrought iron fencing along Seventh Avenue.

MOORISH TOWER
HOTEL LA RIBERA-CARMEL

The early view, taken around 1935, shows the southwest corner of Ocean Avenue and Monte Verde Street with Drever's Inn restaurant on the left and Normandy Inn restaurant on the right. The building in between, which still exists, was architect Robert Stanton's office. The short-lived Drever's Inn opened in 1935, served Southern cooking, and had a taproom. The Monte Verde Inn is now in its location. In the early 1950s, the Normandy Inn restaurant was replaced with the N.B. Flower Shop, designed by Stanton. It is now a retail store.

HOTELS AND RESTAURANTS

The long-running Blue Bird Restaurant and Tea Room, Carmel's oldest tearoom, moved to the south side of Ocean Avenue west of Lincoln Street in the early 1920s. The historic photograph is from 1948. The Blue Bird served "Luncheon, Tea, Dinner." Still a restaurant, it was Scandia Restaurant in the 1950s and remained as such for many years, serving Scandinavian and European specialties. The Norwegian-native proprietors, Arne and Dorthe Kippenes, also owned the longtime Pernille restaurant on San Carlos Street and Sixth Avenue.

Village Corner restaurant, a favorite spot for locals and visitors since it opened in 1946 on the northeast corner of Dolores Street and Sixth Avenue, is seen in the 1960s in the early view. Carmel residents spearheaded a preservation effort that saved it from demolition in 1976. The one-story building with an outdoor seating patio was designed by Hugh Comstock. He used his copyrighted post-adobe construction method to build it.

HOTELS AND RESTAURANTS

CHAPTER 4

DOWNTOWN BUILDINGS

The south side of Ocean Avenue near Lincoln Street looking east is seen around 1909. On the right is Carmel-by-the-Sea Grocery. Next to it is the Carmel Bakery with two second-story bay windows. It is still in business. The community bulletin board is between it and Louis S. Slevin's store to the left. Early on, the town had wooden-plank sidewalks and unpaved dirt roads.

The two buildings in the early view of the south side of Ocean Avenue west of Dolores Street are among Carmel-by-the-Sea's earliest businesses, built around 1902–1903 in the Western false front style. On the left is Thomas Burnight's ice cream, candy store, and bakery. On the right, photographer Louis S. Slevin's store served as the post office and sold postcards, magazines, and curios. There was a community bulletin board between the two. In the later view are, from left to right, an art gallery at the corner, a clothing store, a real estate office, and a jewelry store.

The wood-shingled, Craftsman-style Philip Wilson Building is one of the oldest in downtown. Constructed on the northwest corner of Ocean Avenue and Dolores Street in 1905 for real estate agent Philip Wilson Sr., it has remained a real estate office, though it was also Carmel's first city hall (1917–1927). The March 1922 view, before Carmel's streets were paved, shows a common sight—a vehicle stuck in the dirt roads filled with ruts, giving Ocean Avenue the epithet, "the devil's staircase." (Past image, courtesy of Monterey County Free Libraries, Marina, California.)

The Court of the Golden Bough on the south side of Ocean Avenue between Monte Verde and Lincoln Streets is seen in 1924, the year it was built. It was the brainchild of Edward Kuster, a Los Angeles lawyer interested in music, theater, and architecture who moved to Carmel in 1920. The distinctive Old World, Medieval-style shops transformed downtown Carmel and gave it a defining European appearance. The centerpiece of the commercial complex was the indoor Golden Bough Theater, seen at the back of the courtyard.

The back of the Weavers' Cottage, now popularly known as the beloved candy shop Cottage of Sweets, in business since 1959, is seen in 1924. The one-story, Tudor Revival–style shop with faux half-timbering and a wood-shingled roof resembling thatch was designed by Edward Kuster in 1922 for his wife. It was moved to its current location in 1923, in front of the Golden Bough Theater, where it was expanded with a ticket booth and brick chimney. Businesswoman Emma Otey and builder M.J. Murphy are pictured.

The front of the two-story Golden Bough Theater is on the right in the past view, and the two-story Tudor Revival–style structure built for author Harry Leon Wilson (1867–1939) is in the background of the Court of the Golden Bough. The prominent, popular writer commissioned the building in 1925 for his wife, Helen, who ran a ground-floor flower shop, Bloomin' Basement, and second-story dress shop. The lower level became a popular Bohemian bar and restaurant, Sade's, for many decades, co-owned by actress Kim Novak in the 1980s. It remains a restaurant.

The early view shows the open flagstone courtyard surrounding the Golden Bough Theater's wood door entrance. The theater burned down in May 1935, and only the building façade remains. The entrance now opens to an arcade courtyard with shops. The fire happened after a performance of the play *By Candlelight*. Edward Kuster rebuilt a new Golden Bough Theater on Monte Verde Street between Eighth and Ninth Avenues, and it too burned down in May 1949 after a fateful performance of the same play. A third Golden Bough Theater was built in 1952 in that location, designed by architect James Pruitt.

The one-story, concrete-block Carmel Development Company building with three storefronts was constructed in 1902–1903 on the northwest corner of Ocean Avenue and San Carlos Streets, one of the town's oldest buildings. For seven decades, the right storefront was a grocery store, beginning as Preble Grocery around 1906; then Leidig Brothers, seen in the 1916 photograph; and eventually Kip's from 1937 until 1973, when the space became a retail store. The middle storefront was a hardware store in its early years, now an art gallery.

The Carmel Dairy building's distinctive milk bottle–shaped, two-story tower with a red tile roof "bottle cap" is on the northwest corner of Ocean Avenue and Mission Street. The Wermuth Warehouse and automotive garage is on the left in the photograph taken after 1932. The two-story, fireproof, concrete building (25 feet wide and 184 feet deep) was Monterey Peninsula's first reinforced concrete storage warehouse. Built in 1922, it even had a vault for storing jewelry. The business relocated by 1947. The large commercial building has long since been remodeled, with two ground-floor retail shops.

The Carmel Dairy building's Mission Street side is seen after construction in 1932, commissioned by civic leader Thomas Reardon. The large, Spanish Eclectic–style, mixed-use building with a white stucco exterior, arched display windows, and red tile roof was designed by Guy O. Koepp. The ground-floor Carmel Dairy sold milk until the mid-1940s; its soda fountain operated until the mid-1950s. Home to Mediterranean Market for the next half century, it is now a home furnishings store. Minor decorative changes in 1953 included tile additions to the lower exterior trim and a Mission Street doorway.

The city's public library opened in 1928 at the northeast corner of Ocean Avenue and Lincoln Street and was named in honor of California Supreme Court justice Ralph Chandler Harrison, a bequest from his widow, Ella Reid Harrison. M.J. Murphy designed and constructed it under the supervision of Bay Area architect Bernard Maybeck (1862–1957). Its architectural features include arched windows, a red tile roof, stucco exterior, a Monterey Colonial–style balcony, and flagstone veneer and retaining walls, one with wrought iron rings for securing patrons' pets. The two-story, southern-facing window has a center exit door.

The Spanish Revival–style Carmel Theater, shown in 1957, was designed by noted San Francisco architect A.A. Cantin (1874–1964). It operated from 1936 to 1959 on the southeast corner of Ocean Avenue and Mission Street. Seen across the street from Devendorf Park, the 75-foot-wide by 135-foot-long white stucco building, costing $50,000, had ground-floor arcades with three storefronts, a tower, and a covered balcony, along with red tile roof accents, decorative iron work, and Spanish tile trim on the façade. Designed to fit into Carmel, it had no marquee.

The early view shows the Carmel Theater in 1936 at the southeast corner of Ocean Avenue and Mission Street, now Tiffany & Co. The theater was demolished for construction of the Carmel Plaza, a controversial development covering an entire city block that was ultimately scaled back when it opened in 1960. The outdoor shopping mall has undergone numerous face-lifts through the years; a 2004–2005 remodel brought back a Spanish Colonial Revival style. The historic Doud Building (1932) at the southwest corner of Ocean Avenue and Mission Street is on the right side of both images. (Past image, courtesy of the Monterey County Historical Society.)

The C.H. Grimshaw service station at the northeast corner of San Carlos Street and Sixth Avenue was in business from 1931 to 1944. It was owned and operated by Charles H. Grimshaw and then his son Maurice. The location became the site of a series of now defunct bank branches through the years, including Security Pacific Bank until 1992 and Washington Mutual until 2008; it is now Chase Bank. In the late 1950s, there were seven gas stations in Carmel-by-the-Sea. There are now two.

The location of Joe's Taxi stand, seen in 1948 at the southeast corner of Dolores Street and Sixth Avenue, is now a jewelry store. The taxi company began in the 1930s; it featured 24-hour service, as seen on the roof sign. A 1935 print advertisement boasted: "Trips to all parts . . . Big Sur . . . Seventeen Mile Drive . . . Santa Cruz Big Trees . . . Ride in a Packard. It costs no more." In the modern era of ride-hailing apps, it remains in business as a third-generation, family-owned company. The corner business across the street is now an art gallery.

Businessman L.C. Merrell commissioned the large, two-story, mixed-use Spanish Eclectic–style El Paseo building on the northeast corner of Dolores Street and Seventh Avenue in 1928. The lower floor originally consisted of multiple retail spaces, businesses, services, and offices; in 1990, local restaurateur chef Rich Pèpe opened the Italian restaurant Little Napoli. Former president Barack Obama had a private dinner there during his June 2021 visit to Carmel-by-the-Sea after playing golf in Pebble Beach. (Past image, courtesy of Monterey County Free Libraries, Marina, California.)

El Paseo's architects, Blaine and Olson of Oakland, also designed La Giralda across the street and Hotel La Ribera one block to the west. Together, all three Spanish Eclectic–style buildings constructed in a three-year span (1927–1929) resembled a Spanish hill town rising eastward along Seventh Avenue. El Paseo ("the passageway" in Spanish) has two walkways paved with rough red tiles leading to the central open courtyard surrounded by shops and offices.

The colorful tile fountain at El Paseo's Dolores Street entrance is incorporated into the staircase wall. The custom handmade tiles in the fountain and staircase risers were imported from Spain; the wrought iron was locally fabricated and modeled on drawings made in Spain by the architects. El Paseo is one of the best preserved among Carmel-by-the-Sea's historic downtown buildings and remains virtually unchanged architecturally from when it was constructed. The courtyard is now the outdoor dining patio for Little Napoli restaurant.

DOWNTOWN BUILDINGS

The historic view shows two early storefronts in El Paseo's courtyard, both run by businesswoman Lotta Shipley—Moorish Rug Shop Imports in the back and her real estate office on the right. A 1932 newspaper advertisement announced, "Imports from France, Spain, Italy, Africa . . . Rare old rugs and leather from Morocco."

The center polychrome terra-cotta statue, *The Greeting,* crafted by local artist and sculptor Jo Mora (1876–1947) in 1928, represents a scene from 1840s Mexican California. The original wrought iron work outside the left window and the back hanging light fixture remain.

The Seven Arts Building on the southwest corner of Ocean Avenue and Lincoln Street is seen in the 1930s. The Tudor Revival–style, concrete-block building was commissioned by Bohemian businessman, poet, and thespian Herbert Heron in 1925. Through the 1920s and 1930s, it was used for various literary and cultural enterprises such as Heron's bookshop and printing press, a newspaper office, art gallery, art school, and photographer Edward Weston's studio. It has been home to the eclectic retail store Carmel Bay Company since 1972.

Just south of the Seven Arts Building on Lincoln Street, Herbert Heron commissioned a two-story complex of shops and offices around a brick courtyard with a central Carmel stone fountain. He specifically rented to businesses associated with the seven arts: music, dancing, drama, literature, painting, sculpture, and architecture. Heron was involved with cultural activities all his life. He established Carmel's Shakespeare Festival and the Forest Theater Guild.

La Rambla is a two-story, mixed-use, Spanish Eclectic-style building constructed in 1929 on the west side of Lincoln Street south of Ocean Avenue. The ground floor with large, arched windows had several different businesses in the early years including an antique store, Moorish rug shop, Fredrik Rummelle's artware imports, and Andre's Belle Arts. La Rambla's covered arcade passageway has stairs leading to the second floor with two apartments, and a lower open courtyard, which is now private but was once a longtime outdoor garden shop.

The central arcaded tile passageway with two hanging wrought iron light fixtures is among the distinguishing architectural features of La Rambla, designed by Guy Koepp, who was known for several prominent, now historic buildings and residences in Carmel-by-the-Sea in the 1930s, mostly in Spanish Revival styles, such as the Carmel Dairy (Reardon Building) in 1932 and the Goold Building in 1935, both on Ocean Avenue.

The large Spanish Colonial Revival–style building La Giralda, at the northwest corner of Dolores Street and Seventh Avenue, was designed by Blaine and Olson and featured custom, handcrafted decorative details: tiles, ironwork, and woodwork. Commissioned by Dr. Rudolph Kocher and built in 1927, it began with second-story doctors' offices and a street-level pharmacy. The top floor is now residential, and the ground floor has long been a European restaurant, originally La Bohème, now La Bicyclette. (Past image, courtesy of Monterey County Free Libraries, Marina, California.)

Staniford's Drug Store (1929–1953) on the southwest corner of Ocean Avenue and San Carlos Street opened in 1908 as Carmel-by-the-Sea Drug Store (not to be confused with Carmel Drug Store, which opened across the street in 1910 and is still in business). The original building had been one of Ocean Avenue's oldest, seen in 1937 shortly before it was torn down. Since the mid-1970s, the location has been Laub's Country Store, a retail store selling tourist merchandise.

The north end of the city-owned Sunset Center property is seen in the historic photograph when it was still Sunset School. The Tudor Revival–style school on San Carlos Street near Ninth Avenue was designed in 1925 by Oakland architect John J. Donovan (1876–1949), known for his school architecture expertise. Part of the property is now used as a public parking lot with an electric vehicle charging station, and a portion of it may in the future be converted as a site for possible affordable housing.

Sunset School
Carmel by the Sea, Calif.

The original Sunset School auditorium annex, added to the south of the school in 1931, is now the Sunset Center auditorium. The Gothic Revival–style building on San Carlos Street between Ninth and Tenth Avenues with a steeply pitched, side-gabled roof was designed by architect Columbus J. (C.J.) Ryland (1892–1980) and constructed by M.J. Murphy. The city purchased the property in 1965 for use as a public performing arts venue, home to the world-renowned Bach Festival. It is listed in the National Register of Historic Places.

Two additional classrooms were constructed for the Sunset School in 1929, both designed and built by M.J. Murphy. This is Primary Classroom No. 16–17 on the northwest corner of Mission Street and Tenth Avenue, made to look like a cottage to fit the surrounding residential neighborhood. It is presently used as office space and adult classrooms. Murphy was known as Carmel's official builder for the town's first four decades; he built 350 homes and structures, mostly in Carmel and throughout the Monterey Peninsula.

CHAPTER 5

STREET SCENES

The entrance to downtown Carmel-by-the-Sea at the intersection of Ocean Avenue and Junipero Street looking west toward Carmel Bay is seen in the early 1930s. On the left is M.J. Murphy's lumberyard, which was replaced by the Carmel Plaza in 1960. Devendorf Park and the Carmel Dairy building are on the right.

Carmel City is seen in 1890 from the intersection of what is now Ocean Avenue and Junipero Street looking east with the outline marked for the construction of Ocean Avenue heading up the hill. On the left is Hotel Carmelo, which was built in 1889 and moved in 1903 to Ocean Avenue and Monte Verde Street, where it became the Pine Inn hotel. The current hotel in its location is The Getaway, originally the Village Inn, built in 1954.

The early view shows downtown Carmel-by-the-Sea at the intersection of Ocean Avenue and San Carlos Street looking south toward the Santa Lucia Mountains around 1910. The flagpole and horse-watering trough are seen at the median on the left, now the World War I Memorial. The building on the right, Carmel-by-the-Sea Drug Store, opened in 1908. It was later Staniford's Drug Store until 1953. The location is now a retail shop.

The early photograph, taken before 1922, shows the south side of Ocean Avenue at the intersection of San Carlos Street looking west toward Carmel Bay, with Carmel-by-the-Sea Drug Store on the left. Two auto stages (the Carmel Bus) operated by Charles O. Goold (1871–1931), a pioneering Carmel property owner and businessman, are parked on the street. The stages carried mail and passengers to and from Monterey, five miles to the north, where the Southern Pacific train depot was located.

The north side of Ocean Avenue at San Carlos Street is shown looking west around the 1920s. The Carmel Development Company's flat-roofed, concrete-block building with a stone face, constructed in 1902–1903, is on the right with its three storefronts: a grocery at the corner, a hardware and housewares store in the middle, and Carmel Drug Store to the left, in operation since 1910. Automobile parking along the Ocean Avenue median continued until the early 1940s.

The early view, prior to 1910, shows the north side of Ocean Avenue at San Carlos Street looking east. The one-story Carmel Development Company building and the two-story, wood-shingled Hotel Carmel across the street are seen.

The hotel, built in 1898, burned down in 1931 and was replaced in 1935 by the large, two-story, Spanish Colonial Revival–style building designed by Guy Koepp and constructed by M.J. Murphy on land owned by Charles Goold's family.

The south side of Ocean Avenue at Dolores Street looking east to San Carlos Street in 1921 shows, from right to left, a homeware store, Carmel Realty Company, and more real estate offices. Today, from right to left, are two retail stores; the historic, two-story, Spanish Eclectic–style Las Tiendas building constructed for civic leader and realtor Ray de Yoe in 1930 by architects Swartz & Ryland and built by M.J. Murphy; and the two-story Doud Arcade building commissioned by real estate developer James Doud in 1961.

The north and south sides of Ocean Avenue, looking east from Lincoln Street, are seen around 1910. The wood plank sidewalks and dusty, unpaved roads remained until 1922 when Ocean Avenue was paved—a controversial decision at the time. From right to left on the right side of the historic photograph are Carmel-by-the-Sea Grocery, the historic Carmel Bakery—still in business—and Louis S. Slevin's two-story, Western false front–style store. Cypress trees have replaced some of the pines.

Looking west between Mission and San Carlos Streets, the south side of Ocean Avenue is pictured here in March 1922. The two-story building with two overhanging second-story bay windows (c. 1899)—one of Carmel's oldest structures—was once a paint store then a hardware store. Furniture maker John C. (J.C.) Mikel was owner in the 1920s. The retail shop Adam Fox has been on the ground floor of the building for decades. At the end of the block was the Carmel Garage, later Dick Bruhn men's clothier and now retail. (Past image, courtesy of Monterey County Free Libraries, Marina, California.)

The north and south sides of Ocean Avenue are seen around the late 1920s from the intersection at Dolores Street looking east toward San Carlos Street. Some of the early businesses on the right are the Carmel Meat Market and a real estate and insurance office, later replaced by large two-story structures—Las Tiendas with two prominent ground-floor arcades and the Doud Arcade. On the left, the one-story Carmel Development Company building with three storefront awnings remains.

The 1927 view from the intersection of Ocean Avenue and Dolores Street looking south toward Seventh Avenue shows the most important street socially and civically from the 1920s through the 1950s. The city hall, post office, police station, newspaper offices, meat market, bakery, and restaurants were all located here. The structure in the distance with the flag atop it is the historic T.A. Oakes Building, constructed in 1922, which served as city hall (1927–1946) and the post office (1922–1934) and is now a mixed-use space.

Artistic Shops
border Ocean Ave. at
Carmel by the Sea, Calif.

The south side of Ocean Avenue at Lincoln Street, looking west toward Monte Verde Street, shows the Seven Arts Building and, farther down the street, the Court of the Golden Bough with its historic commercial structures built in the mid-1920s. It was the block that started the European-inspired architectural transformation of Carmel-by-the-Sea, changing it from a nondescript, small Western town into a distinctive place of "beauty and artistry," according to newspaperman and mayor Perry Newberry (1870–1938).

The view of the south side of Ocean Avenue from Monte Verde Street looking east toward Lincoln Street shows the newly constructed Dr. Amelia Gates Building at the corner shortly after it was built in 1928. The two-story, Medieval Revival– style, mixed-use building with clinker brick and faux half-timbering was designed by Gates herself, as was her home on Camino Real in 1922. Parts of the Court of the Golden Bough are seen as well, such as the next-door Seven Arts Shop.

This street scene from the 1940s shows the north side of Ocean Avenue at Dolores Street, looking west toward Lincoln Street. At the corner is the Philip Wilson Jr. (1897–1959) real estate building, established by his father, Philip Wilson Sr., who died in 1943. It is still a real estate office.

Going down the block from right to left in the historic photograph is a hotel, more real estate offices, and De Loe's, a Southern restaurant and cocktail lounge that opened in 1937. Jon Konigshofer designed the interior.

The intersection of Dolores Street and Seventh Avenue looking north toward Ocean Avenue is seen in the 1930s. This block has the highest number of historic buildings in all of downtown Carmel-by-the-Sea. It was the heart of the downtown for several decades (1920s–1950s), with many businesses that served residents. The historic, large, Spanish Revival–style buildings at the corners are La Giralda (left), built in 1927, and El Paseo (right), built in 1928.

The west side of Dolores Street at Seventh Avenue looking north in the 1930s shows the La Giralda building on the corner, with the large two-story Monterey County Trust and Savings Bank, constructed in 1929 in the Spanish Mission Revival style, next to it. The bank became an art museum in the 1960s and then the China Art Center. It is now repurposed as a recording studio. The historic T.A. Oakes and Oakes Buildings, constructed in 1922 and 1923, are next door, now with ground-floor art galleries.

This historic postcard shows the east side of Dolores Street at Seventh Avenue looking north toward Ocean Avenue, with the El Paseo building on the right at the corner. Every structure along this side of the street is historic and was built in the mid- to late 1920s and early 1930s, mostly in European Revival styles. Though the businesses have changed through the years, many retail shops, art galleries, and restaurants are found along this side of Dolores Street.

DOLORES STREET, CARMEL, CALIFORNIA—M38

The historic view from the north side of Ocean Avenue looking toward the south side at Lincoln Street shows street landscaping and cars parked at a diagonal in the center median. In its place in the early 1940s, well-known Bay Area landscape architect Thomas D. Church (1902–1978) designed the stone landscape along Ocean Avenue's median from Monte Verde Street to Junipero Street. Church pioneered modern California landscape design in the 1930s–1970s, emphasizing low maintenance planting for the dry, Mediterranean-like climate.

The south side of Ocean Avenue at Lincoln Street, looking east to Dolores Street in 1938, shows what was the longtime costume jewelry and small home accessories shop Merle's Treasure Chest at the right corner, the two-story Carmel Bakery mid-block, and Mary Dummage's two-story, Pueblo Revival–style building (1931) at the far left corner. It was home to retail store Corner Cupboard for 75-years until 2001, and is now an art gallery. Other present-day businesses include restaurants, retail shops, and a real estate office.

The north side of Ocean Avenue near San Carlos Street looking east is seen around the mid- to late 1930s; the World War I Memorial Arch is in the median. The Goold Building was constructed in 1935 for Charles Goold's family at the location where the Hotel Carmel (1898) stood before it burned down in 1931. The two-story Spanish Colonial Revival building's second floor was the *Carmel Pine Cone* office during the 1980s. The ground floor has been the Coach factory outlet store since the early 1990s.

The view from Ocean Avenue near Torres Street leading into downtown Carmel-by-the-Sea is a familiar sight for locals and visitors as they approach the entrance to the commercial district, coming down the hill looking west to Carmel Bay. The historic photograph shows the north side of Ocean Avenue, the town's main street and its busiest and widest. It runs from Highway 1 in the east to Carmel Beach in the west, going through the center of downtown.

The south side of Ocean Avenue, looking east from Lincoln Street around the 1940s, shows the newly constructed landscaped stone median along Ocean Avenue, the design work of California landscape architect Thomas Church, as part of the beautification of the streets. In the historic view, street parking was at a diagonal rather than parallel to the sidewalk curb as it is today.

The intersection of Ocean Avenue and San Carlos Street, looking west toward Dolores Street in the heart of downtown, has been one of the busiest junctions since the town's earliest days. The road sign in the center median of the early view from 1945 indicates that San Carlos Street, which runs north-south through Carmel, was a truck route at the time. The second sign gives the directions and miles to nearby still-popular destinations: Carmel Mission, Point Lobos, Carmel Highlands, and Monterey.

The outdoor seating patio of Village Corner, on the north side of Sixth Avenue near Dolores Street seen in the 1955 view, shows little has changed in its appearance except the addition of a pergola. An art gallery is still next door. Carmel-by-the-Sea has numerous art galleries; the town began as a Bohemian artists' and writers' colony and has always drawn creative people as residents. The restaurant had been a weekly gathering site for retired cartoonists, illustrators, and artists.

HOUSES

This view from the southern end of Carmel Beach looking east around 1908 shows two of the first homes constructed in southwest Carmel-by-the-Sea. The Tudor Revival–style MacGowan-Cooke House on Thirteenth Avenue near San Antonio Avenue was built in 1905. Farther back is the large Craftsman-style Col. Harold Mack House on the northeast corner of Carmelo Street and Thirteenth Avenue, built in 1907. Both are historic homes.

Soon after Carmel-by-the-Sea was founded, it became a favorite summer vacation getaway for university professors, mostly from Stanford, just under 100 miles to the north. As many of them built redwood bungalows, several blocks of Camino Real became known as Professors' Row. Stanford botany professor George Peirce built his wood-shingled house on the northwest corner of Camino Real and Seventh Avenue around 1910, next door to engineering professor Guido Marx's wood-shingled Foursquare-style home (Holiday House), built in 1905. Both remain to this day.

Pioneering photographer and popular Bohemian Arnold Genthe (1869–1942) lived in Carmel-by-the-Sea from 1905 to 1911, then moved to New York City and opened a photography studio where Dorothea Lange (1895–1965) was his assistant. He designed and built his wood-shingled redwood bungalow on the east side of Camino Real between Tenth and Eleventh Avenues in 1905, the only house there when the early photograph was taken sometime between 1906 and 1911. It had a cellar where Genthe processed film. (Past image, courtesy of Library of Congress, Genthe Collection.)

In 1905, Norwegian-born California artist Christian Jorgensen (1860–1935) built a two-story stone house on the southwest corner of Eighth Avenue and Camino Real for his wife, Angela, an heir to the Ghirardelli chocolate company. The mansion had a 25-foot-tall stone tower and an expansive Pacific Ocean view, two blocks from Carmel Beach. A decade later, Jorgensen leased and then sold the house to Agnes Signor, who made it a boardinghouse and eventually La Playa hotel.

Internationally recognized poet Robinson Jeffers (1887–1962) lived in Carmel from his late 20s until his death. He resided on five acres in Carmel Point overlooking Carmel Bay since 1919 in the granite stone cottage known as Tor House (on the left), built by M.J. Murphy on Ocean View Avenue. After studying stonemasonry, Jeffers constructed the adjacent 40-foot-tall Hawk Tower by hand over the next five years; it was completed in 1924. Both structures are listed in the National Register of Historic Places.

ome of Robinson Jeffers the Poet
Carmel by the Sea, Calif.

zs 382

DISCOVER THOUSANDS OF LOCAL HISTORY BOOKS FEATURING MILLIONS OF VINTAGE IMAGES

Arcadia Publishing, the leading local history publisher in the United States, is committed to making history accessible and meaningful through publishing books that celebrate and preserve the heritage of America's people and places.

Find more books like this at
www.arcadiapublishing.com

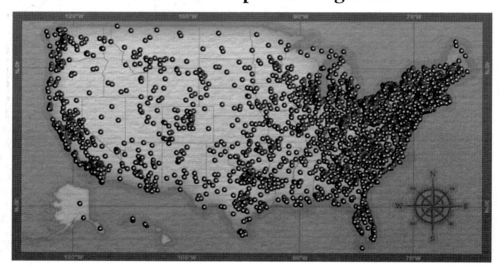

Search for your hometown history, your old stomping grounds, and even your favorite sports team.